UP AMONG THE MOUNTAIN MEN

An outrageous little book of North Pembrokeshire jokes

Collected by Brian John

Greencroft Books

Trefelin, Cilgwyn, Newport, Pembrokeshire
SA42 0QN

Printed in Wales

CONTENTS

The jokes in this collection have come from a wide variety of sources, spoken and written. I thank all the good Pembrokeshire people who have sent material to me over the last few years, and I also acknowledge among my written sources publications by Irvin Cobb, Bennett Cerf, Ashley Halsey, John Aye and others. Very few of the jokes are original, and I am happy for them to be reproduced by others, in keeping with the great tradition of joke collections. As ever, I thank my wife Inger for proof-reading and for telling me what is funny and what is not.

Illustrations: all from Victorian children's comics and illustrated journals

Typesetting and design: Brian John on Apple Mac LC475

Photography and printing: Gwasg Gomer, Llandysul

First edition: 1997

ISBN: 0 905559 74 6

Introduction

This little book is a celebration of the gentle and slightly bizarre humour of Pembrokeshire to the north of the Landsker Line. This area is known to Pembrokeshire people as the Welshry in view of the fact that Welsh was, until recently, the main language of everyday communication. Only 50 years ago the great bulk of parishes to the north of the Landsker had more than eighty percent of Welsh speakers; and it was not at all uncommon to find elderly people in the more remote country districts who could speak no English at all. The Welsh language is still very strong, and after decades of decline there are signs that it is stabilising and even increasing in usage. This is a source of pleasure to all Pembrokeshire people -- including those who do not speak "the language of Heaven" -- since the Welshness of the north is an invaluable part of the county's cultural make-up.

That having been said, we have to recognise that there are two very distinct communities in Pembrokeshire. Those who live in "Little England" to the south of the Landsker are fiercely proud of their English language traditions and their unique culture, just as those who live to the north are proud of their Welshness. Some people in recent years have tried to perpetrate the myths that Pembrokeshire people are all the same, that the Landsker never did exist, and that South Pembrokeshire people are somehow disloyal to Wales if they fail to learn Welsh and adopt Welsh ways. To my entirely biased way of thinking, this is political correctness gone mad. I shall continue to take great delight in political incorrectness by pointing out as frequently as possible that Pembrokeshire's "split personality" is its greatest cultural asset.......

One of the most splendid features of Pembrokeshire is the manner in which each community looks at the other. When I was a child in Haverfordwest I used to hear jovial (and, it has to be said, rather superior) remarks made about "the mountain men" who were all supposed to be a bit slow in the head, uncomfortable when speaking English, and greatly preoccupied with chapels and sheep farming. In contrast, we (nasty little brats that we were) thought of ourselves as men of the world, full of high intelligence and urban sophistication. Now that I live deep in the Welshry I can see something of the attitude of the mountain men to those who have the misfortune to live "down below." The Little Englanders are thought to be arrogant, politically devious, conservative, preoccupied with money, and incapable of understanding what quality of life is all about. Further, it is claimed that they can't sing very well, and that they don't really understand rugby. None of this is true, of course, but we all enjoy our stereotypes.

And it is the stereotype which provides us with most of our local humour. This disreputable little book contains a selection of North Pembrokeshire jokes, classified under a number of headings. Many of the jokes are told by Welsh-speaking Welshmen about themselves. Others (for example, the ones about mean old Welshmen living in hovels up in the hills) are told by Little Englanders about their northern neighbours for no other reason than that they reinforce their stereotypes. And then there are the jokes that North Pembrokeshire people tell about their "Cardi" neighbours, who are reputed to be even more tight-fisted and even more crafty than the Aberdonians in Scotland.

I hope that those who read the jokes on the following pages will enjoy them just as I have enjoyed collecting them. The humour is generally gentle, whimsical and free of malice, and mercifully different from the hard, cruel and crude jokes which we nowadays find in our sophisticated modern media.

My earlier book called "Pembrokeshire Humour" was given a warm welcome by local people when it was published in 1994, and it has now sold almost 4,000 copies. The jokes in this little collection are all new in the sense that I have not used them before; but joke connoisseurs will know that there are no new jokes under the sun, and it is inevitable that readers will recognise some of them as originating somewhere else. But who knows where jokes really come from? They certainly do not come from some gigantic joke factory; and we can be confident that a reasonable proportion of them have sprung from the Pembrokeshire soil and are, in their own way, a celebration of the spirit of the old county.

Brian John **Christmas 1997**

Chapter One

LAUGHING WITH GOD

Like Father Like Son

"Oh no, Sunday again!" grumbled young Eifion. "An' I bet you're goin' to force me to go to Sunday School again. I bet Dad never went to Sunday School when he was a kid."

"Oh yes he did," replied his mother. "He went regularly, and hardly ever missed a Sunday when he was your age."

"Huh!" said Eifion. "All right, I'll go if I have to. But I bet it won't do me no good neither."

Perfectly Reasonable

There weren't all that many Roman Catholics in Fishguard, but the members of the small flock were used to stern discipline. One Friday the priest was going past Gwynfor Murphy's cottage down in Lower Town when he smelt something savoury frying, and when he poked his head round the door there was Gwynfor cooking up a nice pan of sausages for his dinner.

"What's this, Gwynfor?" he remonstrated. "Meat on a Friday? You must do a penance. Bring me a load of wood tomorrow."

Next day Gwynfor turned up with his wheelbarrow and dumped a load of sawdust on the priest's front door-step. The priest was not amused. "Now then, Gwynfor," he said, "you know I asked for a load of wood."

"The way I looks at it," replied Gwynfor, "if sausages is meat, then sawdust is wood."

Beyond Understanding

The Bishop of St David's was having a discussion about life, religion and the universe with a visiting professor of philosophy. "I don't have anything to do with religion," said the professor. "In fact, on principle I refuse to have anything to do with things I do not understand."

"Did you enjoy your breakfast this morning?" asked the Bishop.

"Yes, thank you," replied the professor. "But what has that got to do with religion?"

"Did you try that nice Welsh butter on your toast?"

"Yes, and very tasty it was, too," said the professor, increasingly bewildered.

"Well now, can you explain for me how a black and white cow eating green grass can make white milk that turns into yellow butter?"

"Not exactly, I must admit," replied the academic, with a frown on his brow.

"Then let me advise you, my friend," said the Bishop, "that in future you should have nothing to do with breakfast."

A Blessed Mistake

There was a very posh wedding in St David's Cathedral, by special dispensation of the Bishop. All the crachach were out in force, for the bride was from a prominent local family. The cathedral was packed out with the great and the good. The bridegroom was serving with the Welch Regiment overseas, and the arrangements for the wedding had been made somewhat hastily over the telephone. In checking the details with the young man, the Rural Dean had asked "Are you sure you want hymn number 774?"

"Oh yes," had replied the prospective groom. "I have the hymn-book in front of me right now, and it is exactly the right hymn for such a wonderful occasion."

So that was that. The bridegroom arrived on leave shortly before the start of the wedding service, and all went according to plan until the congregation started to sing hymn number 774. Then, as the assembled voices should have risen to a great crescendo, uncontrollable giggles followed by gales of laughter caused the hymn to be abandoned, and the organist had hysterics and fell off his stool. This is what the congregation was trying to sing:

> Come O Thou traveller unknown,
> Whom still I hold but cannot see,
> My company before is gone,
> And I am left alone with Thee.
> With Thee all night I mean to stay
> And wrestle till the break of day.

Somehow or other the wedding ceremony was completed with the congregation in a state of high euphoria, with the poor bride covered in embarrassment and the groom realising that the Methodist hymn book is not the one normally used in St David's Cathedral.

Doing One's Best

Jenkyn Rees was standing at the Pearly Gates, waiting to be let in. St Peter came out with his big book and asked for his name. "Jenkyn Rees of Pontfaen," replied the new arrival. " I have come to be let in, considerin' that I have been a deacon of Jabez Chapel and have led a good Christian life."

St Peter looked through all the Reeses on his list but could find no Jenkyn Rees of Pontfaen. "You do not appear to be on my list," said the saint. "Are you sure you have come to the right place?"

"Oh yes indeed," said Jenkyn. "Well known I am in the community for my good works and for spreadin' the gospel far and wide."

"That sounds reasonable," conceded the saint. "I might be able to let you in through the Pearly Gates even if you aren't on my list. But I need more convincing. Have you ever done anything great and noble in your life which would qualify you for heaven?"

"Not that I can think of," said Jenkyn. And then he had a sudden thought, and added "But there was the time I went to Belfast for the Baptist mission."

"Very commendable. What happened?"

"Well, I stood in the middle of the Falls Road," said Jenkyn proudly, "and shouted out at the top of my voice that Jesus loves both the Pope and Ian Paisley."

"Even more commendable. Up here we like to see signs of such ecumenical goodwill and tolerance. And when would that have been? Ten or twenty years ago?"

"Oh no indeed," said Jenkyn. "That was about thirty seconds ago."

More Pressing Problems

"And it is written in the Good Book of Revelation" roared the evangelist, "that the world will come to an end on 1st January in the year 2000 AD, and all those who do not repent will rot in hellfire and damnation!"

"A load of old clap-trap," shouted Georgie Griffiths from the back row. "The world will go on and on, an' I'll bet thee half a crown that we will all still be here on 2nd January 2000 AD. You can pay me the day after."

"Aha! I see we have a doubter in our midst," said the evangelist, not used to being disturbed in the middle of the fire and brimstone. "Let me tell you, brother, that when the world really does come to an end as written in the scriptures, you will look pretty stupid, let me tell you."

"Indeed yes," shouted Georgie, beginning to enjoy himself. "If the world does come to an end like you says and when you says, I will surely look pretty stupid. But let me tell you, brother, that that will be the least of me problems!"

Blessed Refreshment

Viscount St David's was paying a visit to the "village city", and had been invited to join a member of the parochial church council and his family for lunch. The Viscount duly turned up, and after a pre-lunch drink in the lounge they all sat down at the dining table. Young Robert, aged five, got on with the Viscount famously, but was somewhat bemused by all the references to "my Lord", "your Lordship" and so forth while his parents bowed and scraped in the presence of the great man.

Robert sat next to the Viscount, and proved to be a very attentive host. Suddenly he whispered very loudly to his mother: "Mam! Mam!" "What is it, my dear?" she asked.

"God wants a pickle."

A Heavenly Miracle

Dafydd was a North Pembrokeshire lad who went to live in Pembroke Dock, having got himself a job in the Dockyard. Within a couple of years he became thoroughly anglicised, and one day he and some of his workmates decided to go to a seance in the Pater Hall.

The famous medium was in a deep trance when the lads arrived, and they were entranced over the next hour or so as she contacted the spirits of many of the dear departed, bringing great comfort to their loved ones. She also established contact with Napoleon, Shakespeare, and King Henry VIII, each of whom spoke words of wisdom to the audience.

Then the medium's husband asked if anyone else in the audience wished to make contact with someone from the spirit world. Dafydd, who had been greatly impressed with the proceedings, immediately spoke up. "Please to speak a few words with Uncle Einon from Maenclochog, who died when a cart-horse sat on him last year."

The medium said she would try to oblige, and went off again into a deep trance. At last, after a breathless pause, the curtains at the back of the stage moved mysteriously, and a muffled voice said: "Hello! Hello! This is Uncle Einon speaking. What do you want to know, my boy?"

"Hello, Uncle Einon," said Dafydd. "Are you alright up there?"

"Oh yes, I can't complain. And how are you?"

"Quite good indeed, thank you. But there's one more question I'd like to ask you, Uncle bach."

"Just you go ahead and ask it, nephew," replied the distant, muffled voice.

"Please to tell me, Uncle Einon, as a good old Welshman from Maenclochog, where the hell did you learn to speak English?"

Chapter Two

LOCAL CHARACTERS

Most Offended

The Dyfed-Powys Police were having a crackdown on the heavy drinkers of the country districts, and having heard that a certain pub in the hills near Maenclochog was "open all hours" the superintendent sent two officers off in a panda car to investigate. Having ascertained that drinking was in full swing round about midnight, the officers observed the pub from a safe distance and waited for the customers to emerge.

Round about 1 am Cllr Davy Davies emerged, none too steady on his feet, and got into his car. Then he drove off down the lane. The panda car set off in hot pursuit and what with all the flashing blue lights and sirens Cllr Davies thought it best to stop. The officer came to the window of the car. "Good morning, Councillor Davies," said the policeman. "May I ask you whether you have been drinking prior to driving off in your car just now?"

"Yes indeed," replied the good councillor. "I had three double whiskies before lunch, three pints of beer this afternoon, and this evening in the pub I had two very nice brandies, six pints of beer, and a vodka or two to finish."

"Oh dear," said the officer. "That sounds like quite a lot of alcohol. I'm afraid I'll have to ask you to take the breathalyser test by blowing into this little tube."

At this Davy got very angry indeed. "My dear fellow," he said. "Do you realise who I am? Councillor Davy Davies is my name. A councillor for thirty years, chairman of the Housing Committee, a respectable citizen and a deacon of Gethsemane for twenty years! I shall have something to say to your superintendent, that's for sure. Most offended I am, that you don't believe what I am telling you!"

Mutual Admiration

Mr Widdington was new to the Fishguard area, and he brought with him something of a reputation as an artist. He set up a little studio and gallery in the town, and did quite well selling rather bad paintings to the tourists.

One day John Evans the photographer arrived at the studio to deliver some prints. "Ah, thank you, my good man," said Widdington. "You must be the chap from down the road who does the photographs." John remained unruffled while the artist looked casually over the prints. After a while Widdington said: "Not to bad at all. In fact quite good. You must have a very good camera."

"Thank you indeed," said John, keeping very cool. "I quite like your paintings too. You must have a very good set of brushes."

Very Stupid Suggestion

Old Bertha Bowen was a tough old widow who lived alone in Castlemorris, not far from Mathry. One day she stepped out from her front door without looking out for the traffic, and was knocked over by a high-speed cyclist. She ended up in a heap in the middle of the road, together with the cyclist and his twisted bicycle. The local solicitor happened to be passing, and as he helped Bertha to her feet he said: "That was a very nasty accident. If you place things in my hands, I am sure I can get you damages."

"There's twp you are, for sure." replied Bertha, very indignant. "It's repairs I needs, not damages!"

Mam Goes to Heaven

Old Mrs Phillips was lame in later life, and needed much assistance from her son Twm Waunbwll in getting about. She was also a cantankerous old soul, who did not suffer fools gladly. She was obsessively careful with money, and passed on this characteristic to Twm also.

When Mam died Twm addressed the assembled company of family, friends and neighbours at the Waunbwll wake. Standing over her coffin he proclaimed: "Listen to me, all you good people! If my Mam owes any of you here a single penny piece, let us settle up this minute, for she will not rest well in the ground with any debts upon her conscience! Speak now, or for ever hold your peace!" And as he glared over his white whiskers at all the mourners nobody was surprised that not a single person spoke up about an unpaid debt.

Afterwards, when the long funeral procession reached the Glandwr Chapel graveyard the mourners discovered that Twm had insisted on his Mam's grave being located just inside the gate. Later he was asked why he had chosen this particular site, upon which he replied "Well, my old Mam was a bit lame, and being by the gate she will have a better chance of getting out quick on Judgement Day."

Chapter Three

ON THE HIGH STREET

Better Than Nothing

A Cardigan chemist was making up a prescription for a customer whom he had never seen before. Having put the twelve purple pills into the little bottle, he turned to the customer and said "There you are, sir. That'll be £4.50 please."

Just then the phone rang, and the chemist turned to answer it. He had a brief conversation, and when he turned round again the customer had taken the bottle of pills, put a 50p piece on the counter, and left the shop. The chemist rushed after him, shouting "Sir! Sir! The price is four pounds fifty, not fifty pence!" But the customer had disappeared without trace.

So the chemist returned to the shop, picked up the fifty pence piece, and tossed it into the till. Shrugging his shoulders, he said with a resigned look on his face "Oh well, I suppose that forty pence profit is better than nothing!"

Nothing But the Best

Mrs Meredith Williams-Evans-Jones was a leading member of the North Pembrokeshire establishment, and tended to do most of her shopping in Knightsbridge. However, she decided that she'd better support the "Backing Pembrokeshire" campaign by doing some local shopping, and she called in to a clothes shop in Fishguard to buy a leather jacket.

Miss Rees, the elderly shop assistant, had her patience sorely tried while the great lady spent thirty minutes choosing a jacket that she liked and then another thirty minutes criticising its stitching, its cut and its design. "You know, my dear," she said finally, "I must be quite sure that this jacket will wear well. Can you guarantee for me that it won't stretch, or crack, or give way when I wear it for a whole day?"

"Madam," said Miss Rees, "I can assure you absolutely that this jacket once held a whole cow together for at least three years!"

Lost Without Trace

Barry John Carpet-man was doing a job for a customer in Fishguard. It was a long job, involving the fitting of wall-to-wall deep pile carpeting in the lounge, dining room and three bedrooms. He had just finished the whole job, and was making a final check that all was well, when he noticed a lump under the new carpet in the middle of the living room floor. He cursed under his breath and thought that he might have dropped his packet of cigarettes while working on his hands and knees. He checked in his pockets, and sure enough the cigarettes were missing.

There was no way he was going to lift the carpet and re-lay it just for a packet of cigarettes, so he jumped up and down on the lump for a while until the carpet was beautifully flat again. Then he gathered up his tools and took them out to his van on the street outside. He took his leave of the good lady of the house, and opened the driver's door of the van. Just then two things happened simultaneously. He saw his packet of cigarettes on the driver's seat, and over his shoulder he heard the housewife call out: "By the way, have you by any chance seen my budgie anywhere?"

Tuppence Worth of Good Stuff

One day a small boy came into Morgan Chemist in Clynderwen. "Well, young man, what can I do for you?" asked Mr Morgan. In reply the small boy held up an empty bottle and said "Please sir, my mam do ask if we can have it filled up with the same again."

Mr Morgan took the bottle and examined it carefully, only to find that the label had long since been washed off. "I'm afraid," said the Chemist, "that there's no label to tell me what the contents were."

"My mam have forgot the name too," said the lad. "But she have been very careful to keep the smell. She says you will find it in the bottle, and here's the money you needs for tuppence worth of it."

Impossibly Fresh

A customer was rummaging through packets of cotton-wool on the display shelf at Davies Chemist in Newport. "Is this cotton-wool really fresh?" she asked.

"Fresh!" replied the shop assistant. "I can assure you, madam, that that cotton-wool was grazing up on Carningli mountain only three weeks ago!"

Chapter Four

LIFE ON THE LAND

The Man for the Job

A wealthy farmer from Maenclochog had a flock of a thousand sheep up on the Presely Hills, and when he began to feel his age he decided that he needed to hire a shepherd to look after them. He advertised in the "Western Telegraph" and had three applicants for the job. One of them was a Pembrokeshire man from Tenby, another was a Carmarthen man from Kidwelly, and the third was a Cardi from Tregaron. He couldn't decide which of the three to hire, so he sent all three up the mountain to see how they got on.

On the second day the Pembrokeshire man came down off the mountain, complaining that he couldn't stand the smell. On the fourth day the Carmarthen man came down, complaining that he couldn't stand the smell either. On the sixth day, the thousand sheep came down.

Size isn't Everything

A big and successful farmer from Texas was on holiday in Pembrokeshire, and one day he went for a drive up Crymych way. He headed off into the wilderness along a minor road with a view to checking out the local livestock, and happened upon an old farmer who was driving five cows back to the farm for the evening milking.

"Hello sir," said the Texan. "Nice little Fresians you got there."

"Not bad indeed," replied Farmer Ifans. "From foreign parts is it? Doing a bit of farming yourself, is it?"

"Cattleman, myself." said the Texan. "Run a thousand head of purebreds on my spread. Not a bad place neither. Do you know, it takes me three days to drive right round it in my car."

"Dammo, there's a pity for you," said the old farmer. "I understand the problem. You know, when I was young I used to have a car like that myself."

Not so Simple

Dilwyn Disaster of Maenclochog had, over the years, lost his wife, his barn, his tractor and his false teeth. At last his friends convinced him of the merits of insurance, and he rang up and asked for the Commercial Union insurance agent to call in and see him. A smartly-dressed young man arrived at the farm in due course and sat down with Dilwyn in the kitchen to discuss matters. "If I insures with your company and me house burns down you pays me two thousand pounds?" asked the old farmer.

"Quite correct," replied the agent. "If that is what your house is worth, that is what you will get."

"Jawch, there's nice," said Dilwyn. "And is it right that you do make enquiries as to how it come to burn down?" "Oh yes, of course. We always make the most exhaustive enquiries in such circumstances."

"Well, there's a pity for you," said Dilwyn, shaking his head wisely. "Just as I thought. I knew there was a catch in it somewhere."

Intelligence in the Dining Room

Once upon a time an American tourist with a very strong Deep South accent went for a meal in the restaurant of the Sergeant's Arms in Eglwyswrw. He was not happy about his soup, and not happy about the service, and not happy about the decor, and made sure that everybody within earshot knew how extremely unhappy he was. A young waiter had to put up with most of the abuse, but he found difficulty in understanding the American's accent and was in any case far happier conversing in Welsh.

Getting no response from the youngster, the American concluded that he was simply stupid. He summoned the innkeeper to his table and said, very loudly: "Say, mister, you look fairly intelligent. Do you speak English?"

"Thank you sir," said the innkeeper. "You do not look so stupid yourself. Do you speak Welsh?"

Nice Day for a Trip

Vince Evans from Eglwyswrw was making his first trip by plane, and was on his way from Heathrow to San Francisco on a Boeing 747. About half-way through the 13-hour flight, and 50,000 feet above the icy wastes of Greenland, Vince was greatly surprised to see Will Thomas from Gwbert coming along the aisle towards him from the non-smokers end of the plane. "Good Lord," said Vince in a loud voice. "Fancy seein' you up here, Will!"

"Good morning, Vince," replied Will, equally surprised. "I thought you would be at Cardigan mart today."

"No no, I'm havin' a bit of a trip to visit my Cousin Wilma. What a nice summers day it is up here, to be sure. An' have you just got on?"

Time for the Treatment

Llew Llaeth was a farmer from Pontfaen who was in Fishguard on market day. He had a worried frown on his face, and decided on the spur of the moment to call in and see the doctor. "Doctor bach," he said when he came into the surgery, "there's worried I am, and I should be most thankful if you will call in and see the wife next time you are passing."

"Only too pleased," said the good doctor. "Is it an urgent matter?"

"Bad business indeed," said Llewelyn. "I has my suspicions that something is wrong. Yesterday morning she got out of bed as usual at four o'clock in the morning and milked the cows and got breakfast for me and the farmhands afore she washed me dirty trousers; then did the farm accounts; churned the milk; fed the chickens and planted the spuds; made the dinner and then ploughed a few fields; mended the tractor; then she made the supper in between repaintin' the livin' room and gettin' some logs in for the fire. About midnight, when she was washin' the dishes, she complained that she felt a bit tired. Very strange business, doctor. Do you think she needs a bottle of that there tonic mixture, or something?"

Fishing Old and New

An old fisherman called Gethin Got Away was fishing peacefully for sewin down near the bridge at Cenarth. His rod and tackle had been inherited from his father, and looked antique; but Gethin saw no reason to change his traditional ways. A young visitor came along and took up his station not far away, with his license in his pocket and with gleaming new modern kit ready for the kill.

"Good evening," said the newcomer. "I gather this is the place. I feel lucky tonight. I've just chucked away my old gear and have gone in for brand new state-of-the-art technology. New super-polyethylene extra-tensile minimum-visibility line, 5th generation high-speed reel, and teflon-coated multiflex fibreglass rod just like the ones they use on the American space programme. Hope you don't mind me mentioning it, but I don't fancy your chances with that obsolete gear you've got there."

Gethin shrugged and got on with his fishing, as did the youngster thirty yards further down the river. The young man caught nothing at all, but when Gethin had stuffed his fifth gleaming silver sewin into his bag he shouted along the river-bank: "Must be off home for dinner. There's nice it's been to meet you. Now there's a funny thing for you -- this evening my old hook just happened to get in the way of five obsolete sewin."

Chapter Five

IN TIMES OF SORROW

No Disrespect

Seamus Murphy was a railway navvy, working on the Pembrokeshire railways in the latter part of the last century. He had been in Pembrokeshire so long that he had married and settled down in a cottage in Letterston with his wife Marged.

One night he staggered in, looking very much the worse for wear with a bandage round his head, a black eye, and his arm in a sling. "Heavens above!" cried Marged. "What on earth have you been up to, Seamus Murphy?"

"Don't ye worry, wife," said Seamus. "I'm just after havin' an argyment wid that fella Billy Murphy."

"Billy Murphy!" shouted Marged. "Do you mean to tell me, Seamus, that you allowed that filthy rotten no-good miserable little man to do all this to you? Why, he's nothin' but a cross-eyed, bandy-legged drunken swine who deserves nothin' better than to rot in ...."

"Husht now, wife," said Seamus in his most soothing voice. "Sure now, ye mustn't speak so disrespectfully of the dead."

In the Midst of Grief

There was great sadness up around Tufton when Farmer Phillips' mule kicked his mother-in-law to death. A tremendous crowd turned out for the funeral, but during the service in the little chapel the minister could not help noticing that nearly all the mourners were men.

After the burial the minister turned to Farmer Phillips and said: "It must be a great consolation to you that your dear mother-in-law was so popular with all your neighbours. It is indeed most moving that so many have taken time off from the harvest to pay their last respects."

"There is nice of you to say so," replied Mr Phillips. "But to tell you the truth, reverend bach, they are here to bid for the mule!"

Pembrokeshire Epitaphs

According to legend, somewhere in a north Pembrokeshire graveyard the following is inscribed upon a tombstone:

"Stop, traveller, stop as you pass by!
As you are now so once was I.
As I am now so you will be;
Prepare yourself to follow me."

Underneath the epitaph an old tramp, who spent a night in the graveyard and who had once been a stone-mason, added the following words:

"To follow you I'm quite content;
But I'm blowed if I know which way you went."

In the graveyard of Bethel Chapel, Mynachlogddu, one may find the tombstone of Twm Carnabwth, reputed to have been the original Rebecca of the Rebecca Riots. His epitaph is as follows:

"No one but God knows
What may happen in one day.
While fetching a cabbage for my dinner,
Death came into my garden and struck me down."

In the Bowen family enclosure in Nevern Churchyard there is the following epitaph to the children of Rev David Griffiths and his wife:

"They tasted of life's bitter cup,
Refused to drink the potion up,
But turned their little heads aside,
Disgusted with the taste - and died."

Chapter Six

EVERYDAY LIFE

Just Not Possible

Billy Jenkins and Glasnant James were looking at the Pentre Ifan cromlech, and wondering about its impressive proportions. "Duw Duw," said Billy. "Most wonderful this is, considering it was built by all them little hairy men back in the Stone Age."

"Yes indeed, I am with you on that point," replied Glasnant. Then, considering himself to be something of an expert in matters archaeological, he added: "Of course, they do say that the building of it was a simple matter. Built by the Irishmen, it was, after they came over in their coracles. To put that big stone up on top of all them pillars, all they needed was a sort of ramp and a thousand Irishmen all pulling the same way."

"There's nonsense you are talking, man," replied Billy. "It must be the fairies what did it. Where in Heaven's name would you find a thousand Irishmen all pulling the same way?"

Quite Safe Thank You

Young Susan, who had never been to Wales before, was lucky enough to get a job as a physics teacher in Ysgol Preseli in Crymych. Off she went at the beginning of the school year, and her mother heard nothing of her for some weeks. The poor woman became more and more concerned, and asked around among her friends in Twickenham as to what conditions might be like in Crymych. Most of them had never even heard of Crymych, and the one friend who had been on a holiday in Pembrokeshire many years before said "Oh dear! I'm not at all sure about Crymych. Most people stay well clear of the place. I think they all speak Welsh up there in the mountains, and burn down holiday cottages, and refuse to speak to the English. And I gather that it always rains, into the bargain, except when it snows."

Mother became almost frantic with worry, and tried over and again to reach her daughter by telephone both at the school and at her digs. Messages eventually found their way through to Susan, who was hard at work and having a wonderful time. To get her mother off her back she sent back a telegram at the end of September as follows: "Working as sorcerer's apprentice. Pay includes three sheep per year. Snow drifts currently only twenty feet thick. Quite safe from the hostile Welsh. Have got digs inside the hill fort."

Advance Planning

Dai Jenkins was a guest at a Silver Wedding anniversary party in the Fishguard Bay Hotel. All those years ago he had been the best man at the wedding of the happy couple, and now he was the guest of honour. No expense was spared, and the bar was full of bottles of all shapes and sizes, containing red and white wine, gin, whisky, lager, sherry, port, beer, and lots of strange spirits he had never seen before. "Duw Duw, this is some party, to be sure!" said Dai, and proceeded to enjoy himself mightily.

The evening was hardly half spent when, much to the surprise of his fellow guests, Dai got to his feet and did the rounds of all those present, bidding each of them an emotional and fond farewell. The host was greatly concerned, and hurried over to Dai's side. "Now then, Dai," he said, "Surely you aren't off home yet, with the evenin' only just gettin' under way?"

"Why no, boy," replied Dai. "I'm not off home for a long while yet. Just being polite, I am. I thought I'd better just say goodnight to all of thee while I still knows thee all!"

No Time for Haste

Mefin Multitude was called in to see the doctor in Goodwick Surgery, ostensibly to have a periodic health check. But the doctor had other things on his mind. "Now then, my friend," he said. "When I delivered your eleventh child the other day I realised that your poor wife is suffering greatly from wear and tear. She is not at all well, and I am worried that if she has another pregnancy the strain might kill her."

"Oh dear," said Mefin. "I never thought of that. I love my wife very dearly, and will never forgive myself if anything happens to her. Take it from me, doctor bach, that if she gets pregnant again I will hang myself. And that's a promise!"

Time moved on, and six months later Mefin's wife confessed to him that she was pregnant yet again. The poor man was distraught, and when she went out shopping he fitted a hook to one of the beams in the kitchen and slung a rope over it. He stood on a chair with the noose around his neck and was ready to jump when a thought came into his head. "Hang on a minute," he said to himself. "Dammo, I might just be hanging the wrong man!"

No Competition

Councillor Billy Stick was Chairman of the County Council, and in the interests of democracy called numerous committee and sub-committee meetings which went on endlessly while all the real decisions were made elsewhere. Most of the committee members turned up dutifully, snoozed unobtrusively while Councillor Stick droned on, and collected their attendance allowances afterwards.

At one singularly unimportant meeting in Cambria House, the Chairman was explaining something very insignificant at great length while the pneumatic drills and pile drivers were hard at work outside the window on the foundations for the new County Hall. After ten minutes of this Councillor Stick shouted out: "This is hopeless! I can't hear myself talk in here!"

"Don't tha worry, Billy," said old Councillor Podge from the back row. "Tha ain't missin' much."

The Wonderful Pills

Poor old Davy had quite a lot wrong with him, and the doctor had considerable difficulty in keeping him alive. On one of his regular visits to the old man as he lay in his bed, the Doctor took out of his bag a most wonderful assortment of tablets of all shapes and sizes.

"Now then Mr James," he said. "I want you to pay great attention to all of this. These big yellow pills are for the heart, and you must take one every eight hours. The little white pills are for your liver, and you take one every morning when you wake up. At lunch-time you take three of these striped capsules for your stomach problem. At tea-time you take two blue tablets for your head-ache, and before you go to sleep you take this little green pill to help the swelling in your knee. Is that all clear?"

"No problem at all, doctor," replied Davy. "But there's wonderful modern medicine is. In the old days we just had the mixture and the pills and the ointment for everything. Now, by God, them tablets is all so clever that they knows exactly where to go when they gets inside!"

Hard Times Indeed

Madoc the Magician came from Fishguard, and he had done very well for himself. With his magic act he was very popular with stage shows and circuses all over South Wales. He specialised in doing tricks with five white doves, which he conjured out of thin air in many different ways, and with equal panache caused them to disappear under handkerchiefs, in boxes, and under top hats.

But times became hard, and for several months Madoc got no bookings at all. The poor man was at his wit's end, but one day he got an urgent telegram from his agent in Cardiff. "Come quick," it said. "Booked with Billy Smart's Circus for six months, starting tomorrow. Big money."

Next day the agent got a telegram back from Madoc. It read as follows. "Damn and blast. Most unfortunate. Have eaten the act."

Chapter Seven

ROMANCE IS ALIVE AND WELL

No Particular Hurry

Colin Casanova, who fancied that he had a bit of style when it came to dealings with the opposite sex, managed to get a date with the gorgeous Myfanwy from Maenclochog. They sat in the corner of the bar room in the Tafarn Sinc in Rosebush, and Colin ordered a nice bottle of wine. They had a glass each, and seeing that Colin's glass was almost empty Myfanwy very kindly offered to top it up for him. She leaned over the table, bottle in hand, displaying her ample bosom. When the glass was about half full Myfanwy said: "Say when." Without batting an eyelid Colin replied: "After the next drink, please, if that's alright with you."

Worth the Effort

Everybody thought he would die, but old Gethin Glasdwr showed remarkable powers of recovery, and with the help of his loving wife Mabel he eventually perked up again, with a bit of colour in his cheeks. Finally, after several months confined to bed, Gethin was able to get up and sit in the garden in the sunshine.

"Duw, Mabel bach," he said as he sat there soaking up the healing warmth, "I shall never forget the loving kindness you have shown me over these long weeks with the sickness. A marvellous wife you have been to me, to be sure. Tell me, where did you get the strength to look after me all this time?"

"It was only right and proper, Gethin bach," Mabel replied. "After all, in these hard times, who else would want an old widow with seven children, five stony acres, and a dry cow?"

Equality in all Things

Ianto and Bethan were a very modern young couple who took over the family farm near Boncath and did very well for themselves. One day Ianto went off to Brian Llewelyn's Emporium in Eglwyswrw and came back with a gleaming red petrol-driven lawn mower.

Bethan was outraged, and made an extremely long speech in which she described the purchase as illogical, impracticable and wasteful when they already had an old hand lawn mower which provided excellent exercise, which was easy to repair, and which had no running costs. "Tell me," she concluded, "what possible reason there can be for spending all that money on a petrol lawn-mower just to cut the front and back lawns?"

"The same reason," said Ianto quietly, "as you had for buying that vacuum cleaner the other day just to clean a couple of little carpets!"

Not too Radical

Young Mrs Wilson had just arrived in Goodwick, and let everybody know that in her home city of Birmingham she had worked as a qualified youth leader. She was very critical of the fact that there was no youth club in the village, and called a public meeting with a view to starting one.

She made an impassioned speech on behalf of the local youngsters. She outlined her imaginative plans, which were well received, and placed great stress on the new methods nowadays used in youth clubs. "No longer can we afford to worship the old and ignore the new!" she said in a state of high excitement. "And we have a duty to our young people to ensure that a young person runs the youth club -- somebody who is young enough to know what teenagers really like to do!"

"And old enough," said Mrs Ebenezer Jones from the front row, "to see that they don't do it."

Perfect Teamwork

Dafydd and Billy were old school friends who had not met for many years. Then they bumped into each other on the street in Fishguard, and decided to pop into the Royal Oak for a pint or two and in order to catch up with each other's news.

Dafydd reported that he had been unhappily married, and that he had been divorced some years back. "Still happily married, I am," replied Billy, "after fifteen years of married bliss."

"Dammo, there's clever. How have you managed that?"

"No problem at all, boy. When me and Myfanwy got married, we talked things over, and I told her I intended to be the strong and dominant partner. We decided that all the **really** important decisions would be left to me. Small everyday decisions just affecting the smooth running of the house was going to be left to the little wife."

"Sounds good," said Dafydd. "And how has things worked out?"

"Perfect, as it happens. We've never had a big argument in all these years. But there's a funny thing. Not a single important decision has come up yet."

A Good Examination

It was morning surgery time in Dr Strangelove's Health Centre in a small North Pembrokeshire town. A pretty girl came into the changing room. As she started to take off her clothes she said: "I don't get it. I tell the doctor my sinuses are bothering me, and he asks me to strip off." A naked blonde, sitting with a little bag on her lap, replied: "My case is even more puzzling. I'm just here to tune the piano."

Good Breeding

Dai Pump was a garage owner who lived in Letterston, and what with the rise and rise of the motor car and greatly increasing petrol sales, he became a wealthy man. The first thing he did was to turn into a Tory Party member, and the second thing he did was to send his daughter Sophie to Cheltenham Ladies College. There, he hoped, she would learn all the social graces and would, in due course, find a nice rich husband.

One day, during the Christmas holidays when Sophie was at home, she was invited to a Christmas Party in Haverfordwest. She came back very late indeed, and Dai and Mrs Dai Pump were awoken by an uncontrollable sobbing downstairs. They rushed down and consoled their daughter, and she related that she had met a very handsome and charming young man who had given her lots to drink, taken her for a ride in his car, and then had his wicked way with her.

Dai Pump was outraged. "Who was this scoundrel, this wolf in sheep's clothing?" he roared. Poor Sophie shamefully admitted that she didn't know where he lived, or what his name was.

Now Dai was even more outraged. "Do you mean to say," he bellowed, "that I has paid for all this expensive education and you **still** don't have the courtesy to ask with whom are you having the pleasure?"

Nothing But the Best

Caradoc Ifans was in love, and called in at the jewellers in Fishguard to buy an engagement ring for his beloved. He had not done such a thing before, and felt rather self-conscious about it; so he leaned over the counter and whispered to the assistant: "Getting engaged I am, and please to sell me a nice gold ring with a pretty stone on it."

"Congratulations sir!" said the assistant. "Would you like the stone to be a diamond? That would be most appropriate."

"Yes indeed, that will be fine."

"And now the ring," added the assistant. "Eighteen carat?"

"No no, you are wrong there," whispered Caradoc, still leaning over the counter. "Can't you tell? Atin' onions I been, on account of bein' very fond of them. The carrots has been very bad this year. Now shall we get back to talkin' about this ring?"

A Most Wonderful Gadget

Myfanwy Evans of Maenclochog had just been to see her boyfriend over in Fishguard, and was returning home after a most pleasurable evening. As she drove, somewhat erratically, through Puncheston, it was her misfortune to be spotted by Constable Williams in his panda car. He indicated for her to pull in, came over to the driver's window, and said "Now then, miss, I would like you just to blow into this little gadget which I have here."

Myfanwy obliged, and when the constable examined his little gadget a happy smile came over his face. "Duw Duw," he said. "That is quite something. You **have** had a stiff one this evening, haven't you?"

Myfanwy blushed prettily. "Quite correct you are, constable," she replied. "But there's a wonderful gadget that is, to be sure. I knew it could tell you I've had a few drinks. But I never knew it could tell you what else I've been up to!"

Sharing is a Beautiful Thing

The new minister was getting to know his little flock, and one afternoon he called in to see Mr and Mrs Jones in their nice villa on the main street in Maenclochog. He was given a warm welcome and accorded the rare privilege of having tea and bara brith in the front lounge.

The three of them sat in comfort, and the minister greatly enjoyed his cup of tea and plate of excellent cake. But as he and the old couple chatted away he became concerned that while her husband tucked in Mrs Jones was not partaking at all in the refreshments. "Now then Mrs Jones," he said. "You have made this wonderful cake and pot of tea. Aren't you going to share it with us?"

"Don't you worry about me, Reverend bach," replied the old lady. "I'll have a bit of tea and cake in a minute, but first I has to wait till Dad have finished with the teeth."

Female Intuition

A visitor called at the front door of Gertie and Dafydd Rees in Newport, one bright and frosty morning in January. "Good morning, madam," he said. "Is your husband at home?"

"No. Out, he is." "May I ask where I might find him?"

"Down on the estuary, by the Iron Bridge." "Ah yes! And might I ask what he doing down there?"

"Well, if the ice is as thick as he thinks it is, he's gone skating. If it's as thin as I thinks it is, he's gone swimming."

Chapter Eight

CARDI JOKES

Just Checking

Evans Egghead, the Cardigan barber, was trying to sell a bottle of his famous hair restorer to a young man who had recently become aware of a bald patch on the back of his head. "Is it quite certain you are that this stuff will do the job for me?" asked the young man.

"Quite certain indeed," replied Mr Evans. "Truth to tell, we have had hundreds of testimonials from satisfied customers who have had a bottle with us in the past."

"Well, in that case," said the Cardi customer, "just you rub a little on your own head and I'll come back again in a week's time to see the result."

Quite a Bargain

A poor old tramp called Micky Mafeking was roaming the streets of Cardigan one frosty winter evening, and having found no place to rest his weary head he called at last at a large detached house. As he knocked at the door he looked about him and noticed that there were various outbuildings around the garden; one of them, he felt sure, would suffice for a night's sleep. At last the lady of the house opened up and looked at him suspiciously.

"Terrible cold it is, to be sure," said Micky. "Please, missus, tuppence for a bed for the night?"

The lady thought for a moment and replied: "I've got all the beds I need. But I likes a bargain and likes to help a travelling man -- you just bring it up for me to have a look what it is like, and maybe we can do business."

Relegated to Deliveries

There was an evangelical campaign going on in Cardigan, and many of the townspeople came to see the error of their ways and turned to the Lord. It so happened that Dai and Wil ran a profitable grocers business in the town; and one day Dai was encouraged by a friend to go along to an evening meeting to hear the great evangelist preach the gospel. He came back home a changed man, bewailing the wickedness of his earlier life and committing himself to a future life of worship and noble deeds.

"Most wonderful it is, to be a saved soul," he said to Wil. "Tomorrow night I am going back to the mission meeting again. You must come with me, Wil, for the Lord is surely calling you to sit at his feet."

"Don't be daft, man," replied Wil. "There's trouble enough with one us us being saved. Diawl, now that you have come over all honest, we'll have to put you on deliveries. Somebody have got to stay normal, so as to do the proper measuring and bagging!"

Time Up

Old Ebeneser Tomos was a faithful member of the Presbyterian Chapel in Cardigan. He attended the morning service regularly on the Sabbath, and regularly placed a penny in the collection plate when it was passed along the pew.

One Sunday he accidentally placed a half crown in the plate, much to the astonishment of the sidesman. Poor Ebeneser was greatly worried by this; so on the next Sabbath day, when the time came for the collection to be taken up, he only pretended to place a coin in the plate. The officiating deacon noticed this, raised his eyebrows, and diplomatically said nothing.

The following week the same thing happened, and so it went on week after week, so that Ebeneser became quite expert at putting nothing in the plate. However, the sidesman was also an expert at his job, and on the thirtieth Sabbath following Ebeneser's terrible mistake he pressed the collecting plate under the old man's nose and said in a theatrical whisper: "Your time is up now, Ebeneser."

Not Intimidated

"Well then," said Johnny Jacket, the Cardigan tailor, to his assistant, "did you collect the money that Mr Mathias Ty Mawr has owed me this last twelvemonth?"

"No sir," replied the boy, looking somewhat dishevelled. "I gave him the Final Reminder and asked him would he kindly pay what he owes us. Then he hit me over the head with the waste-paper basket, kicked me up the backside, twisted my arm, punched my nose and threw me down the steps into the street, where I fell in a puddle, tore my trousers and then got ran over by a man on a motor-bike."

"So that's his attitude, is it?" said Johnny Jacket, furious. "Now just you go straight back again and collect that bill off him. I'll show the bugger that he can't scare me!"

Cardi and Proud of It

A lavish house party was in full swing in Haverfordwest, and the house rang with convivial conversation, laughter and the clink of glasses. In the middle of it all the young daughter of the host thought she discerned a Cardigan accent in the speech of one of the guests, and asked him: "Are you a Cardi, Mr Griffiths?"

The girl's mother overheard this, and afterwards drew her to one side. "That was very undiplomatic of you, Sarah," she said. "If you thought he was a Cardi, why humiliate him? If you thought he was not a Cardi, why insult him?"

Not that Desperate

There was a terrible flood down by the Mwldan in Cardigan, and the swirling muddy waters were so deep that all the residents were forced to take refuge in the upstairs rooms of their houses. Old Mrs Williams was leaning out of her upstairs window in obvious distress when the RNLI lifeboat came floating by on a mercy mission.

"Hello there!" shouted the lifeboatman. "Can we help you?"

"No thank you, bach," said Mrs Williams. "I've already contributed!"

Amusements Galore

A young man from Cardiff arrived in Cenarth for a holiday with an elderly relative. After a few hours he was already bored, and went down to the bridge to see if he could discover where the action was. He met a local fisherman there, who was leaning over the bridge and looking into the swirling water below. "Can you please tell me where the cinema is?" he asked.

"No cinema," said the fisherman.

"Then where do they have the local disco? Or the local night-club?"

"You must be joking, indeed. No such things in Cenarth."

"Do you mean to say there are no amusements at all in this wretched place?" groaned the disappointed visitor.

The local man brightened up immediately. "Oh yes indeed," he said. "Last year Dafydd Dafis fell out of his coracle, he did. Most amusing, it was. The council meets on the first Monday of each month, which is always good for a laugh. And if it's action you are after the Cardigan bus comes in at four o'clock every market day, weather permitting."

Something to Boast About

A few friends were chatting one evening in the bar of The Black Lion. The talk turned to matters of commerce and high finance, and Gwynfor said: "There's one thing I can say, boys, about me place in the business community of Cardigan. Very happy I am to report that I am entirely a self-made man."

"Is it boasting you are," inquired Wynford, "or apologising?"

Just the Girl for a Cardi

John Thomas from Lampeter was head over heels in love with a delectable young lady named Sian. He had to go off on a business trip to Scotland, and became so lovesick without her after a few days that he decided to take drastic measures in order to secure his future. So he telegraphed off a proposal of marriage first thing one Wednesday morning.

He was not at all certain of the reply, and such was his anxiety that he called in at the post-office every hour throughout the day to see if a reply had arrived. At long last, late in the evening, a telegram was delivered to the guest house where he was staying. With feverish excitement he opened it, and uttered a great sigh of relief when he discovered that she had accepted him. He was so overjoyed that he told the owner of the guest-house all about his passionate affair and his long-distance proposal of marriage.

"Huh!" said the proprietor. "I'm not sure I like the sound of this. She has kept you waiting all day for a reply. I should think twice about marrying a girl who would treat me like that."

"No no," replied John. "You has got it all wrong, my friend. Look you now then at this telegram, which says SIAN SAYS YES. Short and to the point, it is. And she never sent it off until the cheap night rate had started. Jawch, not a Cardi penny wasted. Yes indeed, she is just the one for me!"

A Matter of Priorities

Harri Holy Spirit, who owned a little grocery store in Tregaron, was shutting up shop for the day. As he counted the day's takings in the back room, his assistant Alwyn was pottering around the store tidying things away. "Put up the blinds, have you, Alwyn?" he asked.

"Yes. Blinds up nice and tidy."

"Sanded the sugar, have you, Alwyn?"

"Yes sir. And all bagged up ready for tomorrow."

"Watered the vinegar, have you, Alwyn?"

"Yes indeed. And in case you asks, the dates on the eggs is changed and the scales is adjusted three ounces."

"Good, good. Hurry up then and lock up, or late we will be for the prayer meeting at Tabernacle."

First Things First

Old Griff Morgan was a Tregaron grocer who had built up a tidy little business over the years, and he had provided well for his five children. He fell ill, and when at last it was clear that he had not long left in this world, the family gathered around his bed. Opening his eyes, the old man asked in a feeble voice: "Is Dilwyn here?"

"Yes, I am here, Dad," replied the eldest son.
"Is Jenny here?" "Yes, Dad."
"Is Tomos here?" "Yes, father, I am here."
"Is Marged here?" "Here I am, Dad."
"Is Eifion here?" "Yes, Dad."

And with his last gasp the old man shouted out: "Then who the hell is looking after the shop?"

Business is Business

Shortly before Christmas, a commercial traveller was visiting Aberaeron looking for new accounts. He called in at Morris Mars Bar, the confectioner on the main street, and felt that the discussions were going along quite promisingly. With a view to cementing a deal, the rep then said: "Mr Morris, we are offering a free bottle of Scotch whisky as a Christmas gesture this year to every new account."

"Dear me, no," said Mr Morris, looking shocked. "There's wicked it would be for me to take a gift from you like that. They do say that bribery is a terrible thing."

"But is is only a small gift," suggested the commercial traveller, "and if you don't care to take it from me as a gift, pay me a nominal sum for it. Shall we say ten pence?"

"There's nice of you," said Mr Morris, brightening up considerably. "Now that you have made it a business proposition, I sees no objection. Thank you very much, and I'll take three."

Nice and Tidy

Jenkins Blaencwm was walking down the road when he noticed great activity going on in the house of one of his neighbours. He popped his head in through the door and said "Morning, Mr Ifans bach, nice job you are doing stripping off the wallpaper. Redecorating?"

"No, no," replied Mr Ifans, hard at work. "Moving."

Serve them Right

Phillips Physician was called urgently to the Big House early one morning. When he arrived Madam Bowen said "Oh doctor, it's the maid. She's in bed and refuses to get up. I just can't make out what's wrong with her."

"I'd better have a few words with her," said Dr Phillips. So he went upstairs and entered the maid's room. There he found her in bed, looking very miserable. "Now then," he said, "what's the trouble?"

"It's not ill I am," replied the girl. "But I haven's been paid my wages for four weeks, and I'm not getting up until I have been properly paid."

"I must say I don't blame you," said the doctor, and started to take off his clothes. "Doctor, doctor!" cried the girl. "What on earth are you up to?"

"Nothing much," replied Dr Phillips. "But just move over and make room for me. They haven't paid me this last twelvemonth!"

Well worth the Cover

Percy Premium was the representative of a well-known insurance company, and he had the pleasure of working in the Cardigan area. One day he called in unexpectedly on Mr Jones the Draper.

"Good morning, Mr Jones bach," he said. "I have called in to see you about your insurance."

At this, Mr Jones looked somewhat startled, and said with a touch of apprehension in his voice: "About my insurance is it? Well, if you've come to bother me about the last time I got burned out I must tell you that I have no time for such things."

"No no," replied Percy. "Your recent sad loss was sorted out most satisfactorily and your claim was paid in full, as usual. I hope you were satisfied with our service, and that your present policy is adequate to cover you against any future damage by fire?"

"Oh yes indeed, I am well covered, thank you."

"I thought as much. I am here today to ask if you would like to take out a new policy to cover yourself against hurricane damage. We live in windy times, and this new policy will protect you if you suffer damage to your roof, or if a tree falls against your wall, or if your windows are blown in."

"Duw Duw, there's nice," said Mr Jones. "I will have some of that cover if you please. But there is just one thing I am wondering about." He approached Percy and whispered conspiratorially into his ear. "I has to ask you this, being that it is a very important question. How do you start a hurricane?"

Lightening the Burden of Grief

A wealthy Cardigan businessman called Evans Extortionate woke up one morning to find that during the night his dear wife had died. Having quickly ascertained that her soul had indeed gone winging off to Heaven, Evans leapt out of bed and ran to the top of the stairs.

"Mary!" he shouted to the maid who was down in the kitchen. "Come quick to the foot of the stairs! Very urgent if you please!"

"Yes, master!" she cried as she rushed out of the kitchen. "What is it?"

"Only one egg for breakfast this morning, thank you!"

Betrayal of Trust

Captain Morgan of Newport was looking for two new deck hands to accompany him on his next voyage to America. He took on a local man from the Parrog who had wonderful references from a previous employer, and -- at the last minute -- a Cardigan man who had never been to sea before.

Off they went out into the Atlantic, and in the middle of a great gale the Newport deck-hand was swept overboard while crossing the deck with a bucket in his hand.

The Cardi saw what happened, and in due course went to report the sad loss to the captain. "You know that fellow from Newport?" he asked.

"Yes of course," said the captain. "What about him?"

"Something unfortunate has happened."

"Oh dear. And what might that be?"

"Well, he's just gone off with your bucket."

Just Making Sure

Tomos Tanner was careful with his money, and did not often buy animals; but one day he needed to buy a new sheep, so he put in an appearance at Cardigan Mart. He bought a nice ewe at a price which he considered to be greatly inflated, and turned up at the desk to settle up. There was a big queue behind him, but this did not stop him from checking his change four times after he had paid.

"Is there a problem, Mr Tomos bach?" asked the clerk. "Have I not given you the right change?"

"Right it is," replied Mr Tomos, "but only just right."

Too Small an Order

Dicky Jones the grocer decided that he had better move with the times, and so he transformed his little corner shop in Cardigan into a delicatessen. Thereafter he was of course known by the local as Dicky Delicate. As part of his new marketing strategy he went into exotic sandwiches in a big way, and he put a big sign in his window which read: "We make every kind of sandwich in the world."

One of the locals came in at lunch time, and just for fun he asked the shop assistant for a whalemeat sandwich. The assistant was slightly taken aback, and said: "Hang on a minute if you please. I'd better check with the boss."

A minute later she came back in to the shop. "Mr Jones is very sorry," she reported. "But he says he's damned if he's going to cut up a whole whale just for one sandwich."

Dafydd and the Happy Hound

Dafydd Dafis was a cautious farmer who lived in the hills up towards Tregaron. He had a great many sheep and one faithful sheepdog named Gelert. One day a visitor called and noticed that the dog was eating a bone in the corner of the kitchen, next to a broken mirror that was standing against the wall.

"What is that old mirror doing there?" asked the guest. "For your old dog to admire himself, is it?"

"Why no boy," replied Dafydd. "That is part of my modern management system. Profitability is all about holding down the overheads, so they do say. That there mirror is to make Gelert think that he's havin' two bones for his dinner."

Cardi Conversation

Mrs Pritchard Number Six: "Bad job about Mrs Ifans Number Twenty-three. Very poorly. There's weather we are having. They do say she have been out of puff for some time."

Mrs Jones Number Four: "Under two specialists from Withybush, she is."

Mrs Pritchard Number Six: "Poor dab. She must be sinking fast."

Essential Reading

A young Cardi student was studying medicine at Cardiff University, and was finding it a bit of a struggle. So he went to a second-hand bookshop in the city and asked the assistant if there was any book she could recommend to help him towards his degree.

"Oh yes," she replied. "This one here, costing just five pounds, is reputed by all the medical students to do half your work for you."

"Excellent," said the Cardi. "Please to wrap me up two of them."